Building Resilience in Young People

Hannah Dengate
Well-being Lead at Phase, Hitchin

Liz Edge
Director of WIRED (Youth Service)

GROVE BOOKS LIMITED
RIDLEY HALL RD CAMBRIDGE CB3 9HU

Contents

Acknowledgment
Colin Bennett for the support and encouragement during the writing of the booklet.

First Impression June 2021
ISSN 1748-3492
ISBN 978 1 78827 127 1

1

What Does Resilience Mean and Why is it Important?

It was the end of the youth session and Rebecca approached me, with tears in her eyes, her words barely audible, 'It feels like my world has been torn apart.' Not really having experienced much adversity before in her life, Rebecca tried to come to terms with the fact that her parents were getting a divorce. The world she knew had changed forever, and the intense pain she was feeling, the questions she had, the uncertainty that surrounded her future were overwhelming her.

For Rebecca, her crisis really came about with her parents' divorce. For other young people it arises through other disappointments: through loss or bereavement; pain; the heartbreak of their first love; the loneliness of bullying; friendship rejection; unexpected change; feeling betrayed; failure or, most recently, the coronavirus pandemic.

The young people we serve will at some point face adversity

The young people we serve will at some point face adversity, but as those working directly with these young people, we have the opportunity to contribute positively to help them build their resilience, both in the preparation for adversity and during it.

We live in a fast moving and constantly changing world. To thrive, young people need the resilience that gives strength in a time of adversity and hope in a time of despair. Resilience is an essential characteristic for young people to build and develop. We cannot always control the adversities or circumstances that young people will face; however, we can help equip them with tools and understanding so that they can manage their response in a positive way and positively contribute to building their resilience.

How do we do this? How do we build resilience which allows all of us to not only bounce back, but create space to thrive and grow? How do we help young people build faith-filled resilience in their lives to cope with both the storms of life and the everyday ordinary life?

Building resilience is a lifelong journey for us all. The call for action now is to equip young people with the tools and habits to be resilient when adversities arise, so that they are able to draw upon their understanding in order to withstand the storm and go beyond. Our role is to contribute towards building a strong foundation of resilience which allows them to see the opportunities for growth that come when challenges are faced, whilst continuously adding to their foundation and resilience skill set.

The aim of this booklet is to help us understand resilience, and how we can help build resilience in young people. It explores resilience from a biblical perspective and considers what this looks like in practice for both the local church and schools. The focus is on how we can help young people flourish and to be the people God intended them to be. Throughout, there will be practical illustrations and examples of what building resilience through discipleship looks like in practice when working with our local church. We are passionate about helping young people to live life in all its fullness, with them flourishing into resilient, Christlike beings (John 10.10).

How can we help young people be the people God intended them to be?

The first part of this booklet will explore what resilience is, what it looks like and how to build it. Towards the end we will look at the importance of the role of the church and the practical implications for youth work.

Our prayer is that this booklet will be a source of encouragement and a practical tool to support the young people that God has placed around us, helping to equip them to be resilient, and ultimately to flourish to be all that God has created them to be.

Defining Resilience

The term 'resilience' seems to be the latest buzzword to add to conversations around young people and their mental health and well-being. It can be spotted from within our news headlines to government papers, charity slogans to a school's ethos. It is a word that needs to become part of our funding applications and our Sunday sermons. But what does it really mean?

Take a moment to pause and observe the objects around you. If you were asked to pick one of those objects to describe what resilience is, which one would you pick? How would you verbalize why that item is resilient?

Why did you pick that specific item? Is it because it is strong and virtually unbreakable—like a pebble or a stone? Or did you choose an item that could be mouldable and break into smaller pieces like playdough?

Perhaps you are reading this with somebody else and they chose a completely different object from you. As you explain to one another your reasons for choosing that item, did you notice that you both had similar definitions of what resilience means?

No matter what item you chose and the definition you came up with, the reality is that resilience can be understood in a number of different ways and from different perspectives.

The term resilience originates from the Latin word *resiliens,* meaning to spring back. In essence, resilience means being able to bounce back from difficult times and cope with challenges.[1] It is the ability of an individual to function competently in the face of adversity or stress.[2] And a person who can 'resist adversity, cope with uncertainty and recover more successfully from traumatic events or episodes.'[3]

So, what does resilience look like from a biblical perspective? As 2 Cor 4.8–9 says, 'We are hard pressed on every side, but not crushed; perplexed, but not in despair; persecuted, but not abandoned; struck down, but not destroyed.'

Being resilient does not mean that we will not face hard times or disappointments, or that we will not feel the emotions of grief or sadness. These troubles and emotions are part of the journey and it is right to acknowledge the pain and loss included in this process. As John 16.33 states, 'In this world you will have trouble. But take heart, I have overcome the world.' When we face hard times, we can hold onto the strength from God which can help us reach out to him amidst times of challenge and suffering, keeping our eyes fixed on Jesus and not the waves around us.

Resilience is something which can be built

The great news is resilience is something which can be built. It is not a skill that we are given a certain amount of; instead it can be built, grown, developed and exercised. We can learn from our life experiences; much like a muscle, the more it is worked out, the more it grows and the stronger it becomes. Being resilient requires being intentional, especially with the choices made both in ordinary day-to-day living and in hard times. It is about taking the next step, in order to keep moving forward in a healthy way.

Resilience is something that can be cultivated in relationships and communities—it is a lifelong project for us all and a journey we are all on. Therefore, it is not about how much resilience we currently have but about how we build it, in order that young people may be able not only to survive in the face of trials and challenges but even to thrive and flourish, and grow and develop into all God called them to be despite the circumstances they face. It is often through the times of adversity, when it can feel uncomfortable or when we step out of our comfort zones, that we grow. We learn things in the valley that we could not learn on the mountain top. As Brené Brown highlights, it is about learning about how to lean into the discomfort.[4] It is important to cultivate and foster a culture where growth and flexibility are praised, where the process is just as, if not even more, important than the outcome.

There are many times when our young people might have to be resilient, for example: studying for exams, conflict with friends and family, illness, a relationship breakup, facing disappointment, an unexpected setback or, most recently, adapting to living in a global pandemic.

It is not possible to take away troubling situations, or shield a young person from them, but instead we have an opportunity to help young people build the resilience needed to go through these life events. Therefore, it is about equipping them with the skills and tools to be able to manage the situation that is being faced, to have deep roots of resilience to draw on when the storms of life come.

It is important that we help young people develop strong roots of who they are in Christ, that it is in him that they will find their security and through him they are accepted, enabling young people to hold onto the truths and draw upon the promises of God. Even when they face trials and uncertainties, God is the same yesterday, today and forever; he never leaves us or forsakes us. We need to help young people to stand on the truth of God's word, both on the mountain tops and in the valleys. Being rooted in Christ is cultivating resilience through everything we face in our lives.

The Process of Resilience

Whilst bouncing back might be quick, in some cases it is not, and the process requires time and effort. It is important to understand the process that occurs, the growth and learning which can come because of this. Someone's mindset is pivotal in how challenges are faced, and the response chosen. When a growth mindset instead of a fixed mindset is held, change can happen. A growth mindset is to understand that abilities can be developed, and that there is power in 'not yet.'[5]

It is important to develop a culture of growth and flexibility

It is important to develop a culture of growth and flexibility when teaching young people about approaching new situations and challenges. This can be done by focusing on praising the process, the effort and perseverance. This concept of growth is vital in building resilience in young people. Therefore, the importance is not only in bouncing back but also in the journey, the growth and the learning which can take place as a consequence. There are three stages of response to the process of building resilience: the circumstance, the response and the outcome.

First, the circumstance(s) which is faced, such as disappointment, friendship difficulties, loss of a loved one or unexpected change. Secondly, the response that can be made in the face of this situation. This is key to building resilience, as the response we choose makes a difference to the direction we take: whether we are going to choose to stay down or go through the situation by embracing the challenge and looking for solutions. When we cannot necessarily control what is happening, we can challenge ourselves to control our response; to keep trusting God, holding onto his promises. To trust in the face of fear and to keep moving forward in faith knowing that God can bring purpose out of pain and be used for his glory. Our goal is to choose to respond to move forward and not sit in the disappointment or place of despair. Thirdly, the outcome can often be different from what we expect or desire. In the short term we may be feeling negative or even in pain; however, the long-term impact can be positive and hope-filled.

Why is Resilience Important?

Building resilience is important for good mental health and well-being, and psychological strength helps us navigate challenges when they come along. It is important to learn how to build resilience not just in the moment when life is tough, but when life is good, so that when difficulties come, we have the tools and skills in place already.

Think

- As you reflect on your own life experiences, can you think of a time when you have had to be resilient? How can your learning from this inform your practice of supporting a young person going through a difficult time?
- Where might you need to show resilience at the moment?
- What could God be teaching you through this?
- What is the response that you need to make in order to move forward?

2 What Resilience Looks Like

What comes to mind when you think of someone who is resilient? Which characteristics do they show? Maybe it is that they show strength, courage, or are able to bounce back.

This chapter explores Joseph, a biblical character who demonstrates resilience. It has been written in such a way that you could use it as a discussion/Bible study with your youth group to explore how Joseph demonstrated resilience and the implications for our lives today.

The story of Joseph is well-known by many in a contemporary form as a West End stage musical—*Joseph and the Amazing Technicolour Dreamcoat*. However, we need to look beyond the glamour of showbiz and see Joseph not just as a character in a musical but as he is—a significant biblical character who we can learn from, especially on the topic of resilience.

Throughout Joseph's life, he demonstrates resilience in the face of adversity and trauma.[6] There is much wisdom and relevance to be gained from his life. Who we are as people can often be shaped by the difficulties we face and the opportunities for growth and learning that can come in the face of adversity. Joseph was not defeated by the situations that he faced; his life and character, in many ways, is a foreshadow of the life of Christ.

Starter

As a group share what you already know about Joseph and what comes to mind when you think about his life.

Background

Joseph comes from the lineage of Abraham and is the much-loved son of Jacob and Rachel (Jacob's much-loved wife). Jacob had 12 sons; however, he was very fond of Joseph and showed this by the tunic he gave Joseph as a sign of affection and a symbol of a favoured position in the family. This caused Joseph's brothers to show resentment and hatred towards him. This grew stronger when Joseph shared his dreams with his brothers. We can see how Joseph showed resilience in the face of adversity through four Ps: Pit, Potiphar, Prison and Pharaoh.

In the Pit (Gen 37.12–28)

Throughout Joseph's life we see the theme of suffering and disappointment.

How do you think Joseph felt:

- When his brothers threw him into the pit (Gen 37.23–24)?
- Towards his brothers?

Joseph is then sold by his brothers for twenty pieces of silver (the average price for a male slave) and enters a foreign land and culture, separated from his family.

- How do we see Joseph respond to the situation (Gen 39.2–6)?
- How do you think you would feel in this situation?

At Potiphar's (Gen 39.1-20)

Joseph shows that he not only adapts to the situation he found himself in, but thrives, becoming in charge of the household, with Potiphar trusting Joseph and recognizing his skills and gifts. Joseph had not lost hope and, most importantly, 'The Lord was with Joseph,' which Potiphar recognized.

In Gen 39.11–20 we see Joseph face suffering and disappointment once again. Joseph had risen in Potiphar's house, only to fall again by false blame. We can see the contrast in Joseph's living conditions; he had gone from being in the house of his Egyptian master, to his home becoming prison. However, once again, Joseph demonstrates the qualities of adaptation and flexibility, and we see him adjust in the new situation he is placed in. Joseph once again thrives in the environment in which he has been placed and ascends to a position of authority in prison, just as he had done in Potiphar's house.

Adapting to new situations is of great significance in relation to being able to be resilient, and is something which can be observed in Joseph's life. Joseph is learning, growing and adapting in the face of adversity.

- Can you think of a time when you have been in a situation where you have had to adapt?
- What did you have to change in order to adapt?
- How well do you think you adapted?
- What have you learnt from that situation?

In Prison (Genesis 40)

Whilst Joseph was in prison, once again his skills, abilities and character are noticed. During Joseph's time in prison, one significant event is recorded: the interpretation of the dreams for both the cupbearer and baker who are put into the his care while in prison (Gen 40. 9–19). Joseph was not limited by his surroundings and sought to use his gifts to serve God in helping those around him. Joseph uses the situation that he is in for a purpose and to be able to bring glory to God.

- How can we use the skills and gifts that God has given us in the places we find ourselves in?

As a result of interpreting the cupbearer's dream favourably, Joseph pleads 'Remember me,' 'Show me kindness' and 'Get me out' (Gen 40.14). However, despite this, 'The chief cupbearer, did not remember Joseph' and failed to do anything for him (Gen 40.23).

Here again we see the knockback of disappointment that Joseph faced: his hope of being able to get out is taken away. Feeling forgotten and still in what feels a hopeless situation, Joseph is now faced with waiting. Yet Joseph does not lose his faith and hope in God.

- When might we feel disappointment?
- How can it feel when we feel forgotten?
- How can we respond in these situations?
- We see that Joseph had to wait. Can you think of a time when you have had to wait? How did you find it? Was there anything that you learnt during the time of waiting?

Sometimes people let us down and things do not work out the way we want them to, but God does not forget us. We may feel alone, but we are never alone—we can see that throughout all this 'The Lord was with Joseph.' Joseph does not lose hope; he does not complain or demonstrate resentment. Joseph chooses to remain faithful to God and continues to put his trust and hope in him, even in the face of adversity.

- How can we choose to continue to trust Jesus when we face disappointments and setbacks?
- How can we help each other to be able to hold onto hope in times of adversity?

This summary of Joseph's life demonstrates how despite facing suffering, disappointment and setbacks he does not lose his faith and confidence in God, providing an example of how to deal with adversity.

Pharaoh's Dream (Genesis 41)

Through Joseph remaining faithful to God in his time of waiting, he held onto his purpose. In this chapter we see Joseph interpreting the Pharaoh's dream correctly. Pharaoh could see evidently that the Lord was with Joseph, and because of this Pharaoh put Joseph in charge of the land of Egypt. God used Joseph's pain and suffering for his glory and purposes.

- Can you think of a time when God has used suffering for his purposes in your life?

Forgiveness (Genesis 45)

Forgiveness is an important factor of building resilience. From Joseph's life we can also learn about forgiveness, and the impact that this can have. We see forgiveness between Joseph and his brothers being outworked in chapter 45. The way in which Joseph demonstrates forgiving his brothers gives us a glimpse of Christ's forgiveness towards us. Joseph suffered at the hands of his brothers, but did not give in to bitterness or let hatred or resentment shape his life. Instead, Joseph chose to forgive his brothers. Joseph had a choice to take revenge, to harbour resentment or to forgive. Yet Joseph saw that his suffering had been part of God's plan and purposes.

- Is there someone who you need to forgive, or need to take on that first step in the journey of forgiveness?

Joseph is a man with a purpose for his life, holding on to his confidence in God. Joseph is aware of his God-given skills and abilities and uses them to bring about kingdom purposes for God's glory. Joseph holds on to this throughout the suffering, disappointment and adversity faced.

God uses the adversity in Joseph's life to shape him and mould his character to become more Christlike. God uses the injustices in Joseph's life for his glory and uses his circumstances to bring about his purpose. Joseph learns to wait on God's timing and chooses to put his hope and confidence in God alone, who then uses Joseph's hardships for preparation to do something much greater than he could have imagined.

3 What Makes and Breaks Resilience?

In our instantaneous culture we are often searching for the one-click button that quickly makes us into a resilient person. We can often find our attention spans shortening, quickly becoming frustrated at 30-second adverts before a YouTube clip or the eye roll at yet another delayed train. We are becoming less patient in our faith and desiring a more instant God, wanting our prayers to be answered in the moment, not having to wait around. The reality is, the button simply does not exist. Our Christian faith is rooted in forgiveness, patience and honour. Resilience is the key that locks these components together, enabling us to build resilience continuously throughout our lives by facing adversities. Yet, what are these adversities which make and break resilience for us and our younger generations?

Facing Adversities from a Holistic Perspective

Young people face all sorts of adversities in their lives. These can either make or break their resilience. This could be anything from family breakdown to bullying at school; being diagnosed with a long-term illness to the bereavement of a grandparent. Adolescence is a time of rapid biological, emotional and social changes and has been referred to as an emotional assault course.[7] The physiological factors of racing hormones, starting menstruation and changing body shape are enough to test a person's resilience, let alone going through the school system of primary to secondary, sitting exams and constantly being asked, 'What do you want to be when you grow up?'

Identifying emotions is a key part in developing a person's emotional intelligence—the ability to recognize, understand and manage our own emotions. Developing these skills is a lifelong process and fundamental to living an enriching life.[8] By identifying and understanding our emotions, we are able to build a strong foundation of resilience.

It is essential that young people do not see emotions as a weakness, but instead learn to understand and express them in a healthy way. Our emotions play a significant role in our lives and, as Christians, we believe emotions are a part of our human and divine nature. As youth workers, we have a responsibility to break down cultural barriers and help young people engage with their emotions, which at times may mean helping them learn to work through or sit with hard or difficult emotions such as loss, disappointment or sadness.

As we follow Christ, we see he is not an emotionless robot, but a man of sorrow and a man of joy. Throughout Scripture we see Jesus expressing his emotions, from sadness to compassion, laughter to joy. From being tested in the wilderness (Matt 4.1–11) to being filled with sorrow in the garden of Gethsemane, Christ felt his feelings and we too must learn to do the same (Matt 26.36–39).

One of the challenges we face as youth workers is to view these adversities from a wider holistic perspective, not excluding our spirituality but instead fusing together knowledge and beliefs.

Case Study

Kevin was referred for one-to-one support as he was displaying antisocial behaviour in school and not communicating with school support staff. He met with his youth worker mentor once a week in school to explore his thoughts and feelings. The sessions involved discussions around his behaviour and elements of fun such as playing Uno. Kevin's home life was unsettled, and he ended up being taken into foster care during the mentoring relationship. Mentoring became a key platform to allow him to build on his resilience foundation. It gave him space to be honest and identify his emotions. It also allowed a time of laughter and freedom. Kevin displayed resilience as even though his school and home life were constantly changing, he attended mentoring sessions each week. He committed to the relationship and recognized it was a support mechanism put in place for him. We often think of resilience being the final result in a destination but rather, like Kevin, resilience is learnt through the commitment of the journey.

Are Adversities Always Negative?

Often, we view adversity through the lens of negativity—a circumstance that is put on us without our consent. Yet, adversity can also be positive. It can help us grow and develop into healthier, more Christlike beings. The anxieties a young person experiences when joining the Sunday worship band, or changing from one youth group to another, can be completely normal. The anxious thoughts and feelings they are experiencing can be a positive learning opportunity, rather than an instantaneous and long-lasting fear.

Adversities do not need to be ignored and young people do not need to be sheltered from all of them. What young people need is to learn how to cope with them and, when needed, ask for help. This can be achieved through continual support networks such as parents and carers, their peers, and fellow church members. What helps to build resilience is creating a culture of social support and, for this, the church plays a key role. Meeting others at youth events, social gatherings, mentoring programmes and the opportunities to build peer and intergenerational relationships all help exercise the muscle of resilience.

Is Resilience Static?

Resilience is not static. It can change over time due to experiences and circumstances we and our communities directly and indirectly face. It is not a vulnerability or weakness, but rather a strength which everyone can continuously develop. A helpful way to understand resilience is to see it as a competence which can be actively developed, taught, practiced, demonstrated and deployed.[9]

The Resilience Framework suggests a number of ideas and practices which promote resilience and offer ways in which it can be practised and developed.[10] First, the basics include a healthy diet, exercise and sleep. Secondly, belonging—the importance for children and young people to understand their place in the world and the building of healthy relationships. Thirdly, learning—for example having a mentor or developing skills. Fourthly, coping skills—such as problem solving and understanding how to manage emotions. Lastly, core self—involving helping the young person to foster their talents and instil a sense of hope.

Building resilience is not a linear and quick process. It takes time to build and nurture and it continuously grows and develops. Resilience goes far beyond making or breaking, and rather becomes a concept which grows deeper inside of us all, in conjunction with the Holy Spirit.

Jesus' Resilience

Jesus' ministry had a positive response on those around him, even though it was littered with adversities. He had to cope with those circumstances whilst holding the gigantic weight of his calling. Jesus demonstrated that in the midst of challenges, anxieties and often pain, we can thrive. Our faith is built on a resilient Messiah who did not shy away from hard things, but instead leaned into them and worked in tune with God to fulfil his life.

As Christians our faith can range from exhilarating moments of certainty to a valley of questioning and disbelief. Yet, it is through this journey that we make resilience a part of our faith and continue to lean into the discomfort, trusting that our loving God is with us each step of the way.

What makes resilience is how a person reacts and deals with the circumstances that they voluntarily or involuntarily face. Do they crumble and not bounce back, or do they face the adversity of the challenge like Jesus and Joseph did?

Think

- How do you make or create your own resilience?
- What adversities have your youth group or congregation faced which have led to becoming a resilient group or community?
- How have young people demonstrated their resilience to you as their leader?
- How did your preconceptions of young people's resilience impact your ministry? Why did it change?

4 How Do I Build Resilience in Young People?

As explained in previous chapters, resilience and positive well-being are unequivocally connected. Those who minister to young people are in a prime position to support them to manage adversities during adolescence. There are some key roots which can help build resilience, and these are going to be explored further.

Purpose

Being able to find purpose is a powerful source of motivation and has been shown to be a reliable marker of flourishing, thriving, life satisfaction and resilience. Purpose helps to keep us motivated to keep going, and to hold onto the 'Why.'

Rick Warren argues in his well-known book *The Purpose Driven Life* that 'Nothing matters more than knowing God's purpose for your life, and nothing can compensate for not knowing it—not success, wealth or fame.[11]

Adolescence has been shown to be a significant time for formulating and cultivating a sense of purpose. Research by Youthscape has shown that the second most important priority for 76% of young people is the 'feeling that they have achieved something that matters.'[12]

It is essential that purpose is fostered and developed in young people in order to help build their resilience, so that in the hard times this can be held onto. Developing and maintaining a sense of purpose provides a strategy for bouncing back and being able to move forwards, by being able to stay focused on the purpose held.

A crucial part of young people working out their purpose is helping them to identify their God-given skills, talents and what it is that they are passionate about. All these help towards young people being able to recognize how they can contribute to their communities around them, and the role they have to play.

Case Study

A story of one young person called Lucy demonstrates what it is to have a clear sense of purpose. Her purpose is to 'raise money for people who have no access to clean drinking water.' When asked what this means to her, she says, 'I do this because I think it's what God wants the world to be like. He doesn't want people to drink dirty water, so I'm trying to change this. I think it's one of the most important things in my life. It's so unfair. Homeless people might find a home, but these people aren't safe with the water they have. Knowing I've now raised enough to provide water for a whole village makes me surprised, happy and flabbergasted. I think I am the child in the starfish story.'

'I think it's one of the most important things for my life.' This shows the significance that the role of purpose can have, and the importance of one's life. Having this sense of purpose is something which needs to be fostered and cultivated.

Think

- How do we help young people identify what they are passionate about and recognize the gifts and skills that God has given them?
- How do we help them work out their God-given purpose?
- How can we give opportunities to young people to use their gifts and skills within the church?

Support

We are all created with a desire to connect with others; we flourish and thrive when we do. We were not designed to do this journey of life on our own; we need others around us to encourage us, to pray, to cheer us on and be that listening ear. We see throughout Scripture that the theme of relationships is demonstrated. We were designed for connecting with one another by a God who himself in very nature loves connection. This connection is displayed fully in the Trinity which models an understanding of relationships. God exists as three distinct persons, Father, Son and Holy Spirit, yet one God.

Being resilient is not about being invincible, but instead knowing when to reach out to others, to let people in, and have people who will remind us to keep going when life is tough. Allowing people in takes courage and vulnerability but it is an important part of building resilience.

Simon Thomas (a Christian TV presenter and co-author of *The Well-being Journey*) talks about the role of social support within the church after the sudden passing of his wife, 'That's where my support has come from, because that's what church is about, it's about community, we sit down, we chat, we pray.'[13] This experience demonstrates the significance and importance of the role of social support, especially when it is found within the church community.

National statistics have shown that one of the main challenges that young people face today is 'loneliness, someone to rely on and a lack of sense of belonging to their neighbourhood.'[14] This highlights the role that isolation and loneliness play on mental well-being in young people and how destructive it can be in relation to building resilience. Young people in the twenty-first century yearn to be connected but are feeling isolated and lonely, despite platforms being available for connection. The feeling of loneliness has increased during the pandemic with 87% of respondents to a Young Minds survey agreeing that they felt lonely or isolated during the lockdown period.[15] As loneliness continues to rise, how can we support young people in building their resilience?

Three important elements that can help young people have a support network and build their resilience are:

Ask for help—have the courage to ask for help; develop a strong network of people who you can be honest with and who will go on the journey with you. Reach out to God, be vulnerable and share with him your deepest fears and worries; turn to him in prayer.

Build in time with people—build relationships and friendships with those who will be with you during the joys and challenges of life, who will cheer you on and who will build you up.

Create a culture of being resilient—look out for one another, supporting and praying for each other, having the courage to be vulnerable and to let each other in on the journey, creating a sense of belonging and support amongst our church communities.

Think

- How can you create a sense of belonging in your youth group?
- In the times we find ourselves in, how can you help the young people you work with to connect with one another in meaningful ways?
- How can you help the young people build strategies which are sustainable throughout their lives?

Self-care

As much as the self-care movement has been highjacked by marketing companies, the essence of the concept is vital for surviving and thriving. By looking after our physical and mental well-being we are providing ourselves with a strong foundation to face challenging and difficult situations in a healthier way.

When our bodies have the energy and nourishment they need, along with being well rested, they give us the strength (mentally and physically) to be able to make key choices and decisions in a healthy way. God cares for our whole being; by providing young people with a holistic approach to our well-being, we can empower them to value themselves, which honours our creator. It is so important to look after ourselves; there is only one of us, and we cannot help others, or give to others, if we are not looking after ourselves. When we value ourselves by engaging in self-care, we can not only survive, but thrive in life.

Some practical ways include the importance of sleep, rest and exercise. Getting regular exercise can impact our mood, and our well-being. It is important to help young people think about what activities give them joy! What hobbies do they enjoy doing? Building and incorporating these into their routine can help to positively impact their well-being. When we do these activities, they are life giving and fill us up again, so that we are able to have energy to help others.

Our thoughts can be very powerful and can affect the way in which we see things. Being able to see things from different perspectives and angles can help how our thoughts impact our feelings. One way in which we can do this is through gratitude. By having a thankful heart, we can turn our worries into prayers and focus on how God may see the situation.

All these proactive actions of self-care and creating healthy habits can help in building resilience. If the habits are in place, then when the storms of life come, it can help us to face the problem in a healthy way.

Think

- What three healthy habits could young people put in place to build good self-care?
- Ask the young people to reflect upon the activities which bring them joy and refill them.
- As a youth group, how can you practise the habit of gratitude together?

5 The Role of the Church

Many young people are exploring what a Christian faith can look like, what it means for them and how it can guide their lives. They are learning from those around them and figuring out what being a Christian actually means. For some it is a strong foundation that they have decided to commit to, and for others it is a mere habit that their parents want to instil in them.

Community-level characteristics play a role in fostering and maintaining resilience. If the church is a community, how does it fit into this? What does a resilient church look like?

Resilience Through the Church

Church must operate within a society whilst trying to uphold its own values and ethos. It needs to be active and alive in what it does and engage the multifaceted tool of resilience to achieve these aims. The body of Christ needs the competence of resilience to outwork its kingdom vision. There is a responsibility on the church as a whole and the individuals within it to participate in building resilience—in ourselves, in our youth groups, in our wider congregation and community.

Our aim as practitioners working with young people in the twenty-first century needs to be focused on helping young people build strong and deep roots, so that they remain rooted when the challenges and storms of life come their way. This should enable them to develop a healthy root system, which is ultimately rooted in Christ. What does an outworking of this look like practically in our youth work today so that we can help young people to be resilient and flourish?

As the church and youth workers, it is crucial we find ways of helping young people to create a sense of belonging and connectedness, and ultimately the opportunity to know the one who created them and wants them to be in relationship with him. There needs to be a development of true communities—the church has an opportunity to provide this by being a place which helps young people to feel like they have a sense of belonging, they are valued and are in a safe place where difficult questions can be asked. Having a place to belong and feeling valued are factors that contribute towards building resilience.

Below are four practical ways to help create a culture of building resilient young people.

Creating a Space of Support and Safety

God is relational, which we see reflected by the Trinity itself, and God wants us to be in relationship with one another. Creating a culture in which support can be found is essential for young people as they navigate all aspects of their lives. Having the support in place around young people is a factor in helping to build resilience, and helps them feel like they have a sense of belonging. Whilst the sense of belonging can seem like a small thing when viewed as an isolated concept, it can have such an impact on a young person's well-being. The church is in a position where it has the opportunity to provide this through youth groups. These can be spaces where opportunities are created for young people to know that they are supported in all that they are facing.

Case Study

Holly and I were standing in the youth room with her friend. When her friend asked, 'What is this room?' Holly said, 'It is a place where we meet, it is a safe place, a place where I know I can come and just be.' The youth room became a safe place, a place where the young people knew they belonged, where a sense of community was found and a place for mission to occur, as they felt they could bring their friends into that space.

If you do not have a tangible room, the culture of support and safety can flow from when and wherever you meet together. The space created is a place in which the culture reflects the character of Christ through virtues such as kindness and compassion demonstrated by both the young people and leaders. The idea is that through this community young people see and experience the impact of the gospel, pointing them towards the hope that we have and the difference that this can make in their lives.

The energy or vibe which is felt when in the presence of certain people or in a designated space can create a sense of belonging and community which subsequently helps build resilience. A space does not always have to be a physical room. Being physically present with a young person can create a physical and emotional aura of safety and connection.

Mentoring

Another vital way of helping to build resilience is through the role of mentoring. Mentoring relationships allow honesty and openness to be fostered, whereby a stable and meaningful relationship can be cultivated, one that is much desired in this culture. Mentoring also allows the unique opportunity for intergenerational relationships to develop, again reinforcing family figures—such as father, mother or even grandparent—for young people and where wisdom and experiences can be shared.

Research by Southwick and Charney has demonstrated that young people who have a mentor are more likely to display resilience.[16] Research by Fuller Youth Institute suggests that in order for faith to stick, there is a 5:1 ratio—if each young person has five adults around them, whether that is family members or friends, they are more likely to 'stick' at their faith.[17] The church as a community has an opportunity to be able to provide mentor figures for young people.

It is frequently reflected at the end of mentoring programmes that a helpful difference is often the power of simply creating an environment in which the young person can be listened to.

Mentoring relationships can help give young people the skills and tools that they need to put strategies in place that will help them overcome the challenges and obstacles that they face with the pressures that come their way from the culture that they live in. Mentoring relationships show the commitment to walk with the broken, show compassion and grace, and to speak the truth of the gospel message into their lives at that particular time in life.

Mentoring relationships not only provide a space of support but also a space to see the potential in someone else, helping them to flourish into the person that God has created them to be. Mentoring relationships can help develop purpose in a young person and help them to identify their skills, giftings and abilities which can be used for advancing God's kingdom. In mentoring relationships, potential can be seen and developed in the mentee, allowing them to flourish and thrive as children of God.

Mentoring gives the young person the opportunity to step outside of their comfort zone, into new situations, and learn in a safe and supported environment. Even if the mentee does not succeed, learning from failure is an important aspect of developing resilience. It is crucial that we allow young people not to be afraid of failing—instead choosing to see it as an opportunity for growth and learning—and use these opportunities to teach young people how they can learn from failure and the disappointments of life, helping them to be adaptable and flexible in their thinking, looking for solutions and ultimately helping them to become more resilient.

Case Study

Carl was referred for one-to-one mentoring due to his low mood and lack of concentration in class. At the start of the block of six one-hour weekly sessions, Carl reflected how he simply wanted 'a safe space to be heard in.' By the end of the sessions, Carl shared how he was grateful for this safe space and left feeling calmer and more able to focus in class. By being offered a safe environment, cultivated with honesty and laughter, Carl was able to achieve his goal of being able to concentrate better and lift his mood.

Serving the Local Schools

As the church, we have a great opportunity to be able to serve the local schools, both primary and secondary. The topic of well-being and resilience is something which can be spoken into. Schools across the UK are seeing many challenges such as budget cuts, a changing syllabus, and an increase in mental health issues. This means that the pressures are more for those working in school. Through building relationships with local schools and seeing what the need is we are able to find ways to serve them. Promoting good well-being, mental health and resilience is something which is a huge focus for schools. We are to see young people holistically; this is an area which cannot be ignored.

What does it look like to serve the local schools around you? How can your church serve schools through ways such as mentoring? Serve from a place of what you are passionate about, what your strengths are and offer hope through who you are. I was once asked the question, '*What do you want to bring into the room?*' As we have the opportunity to serve the local schools, what is it that we want to bring? To think intentionally about this, how can you bring that fragrance, that aroma of Christ, and how can you demonstrate the hope that we have in Christ, and that there is reason to choose to hope even in the storms of life?

Three Ps to consider when thinking about how to serve your local schools are Purpose, Partner and Passion.[18] Purpose: why is it that you do what you do? Partner: who can you partner with? Are there other local churches or organizations with whom you could serve the schools? Passion: what is it that you are passionate about? What are some of the strengths that you can use to serve the schools near you?

Teaching Topics

The mention of a topic gives permission to have a conversation. An important aspect of discipleship is the topics being taught and discussed with young people, topics such as suffering, forgiveness, apologetics and mental health, all of which will allow young people to wrestle with the challenges and the big questions that may come their way. It is often much easier to learn about these topics when out of the storm than when in, therefore it is about preparing young people and giving them a strong foundation to be able to stand upon, and from which they are able to draw.

Life is not always going to be easy, and the Christian life is certainly not always going to be easy, therefore it is important that young people know that God is still good in the tough times; he is the same God on the mountain tops as he is in the valleys. They can choose to keep trusting God, holding onto his promises in the face of disappointment, to choose to trust in the face of fear, to choose to keep moving forward in faith. A good understanding of suffering can impact upon the level of resilience.

It is crucial that space is being created for topics such as suffering and forgiveness to be discussed. God can take pain and suffering and use it for his good. By building teaching about suffering into our discipleship programmes, we can help prepare the young people for when the times of suffering and difficulty come, giving them the understanding and skills to be able to draw upon when the challenges and difficulties come.

While the topic of forgiveness is a sensitive one and can be hard to talk about, it is essential to discuss. Those who are taught the skills of how to forgive are shown to be able to forgive, and this increases their resilience.[19] Forgiveness is necessary for a person's mental and emotional well-being. As youth workers, we want to help young people to work through forgiveness so that they can grow to become more like Christ, bringing freedom, and helping young people to live life to the full so they are not held back by unforgiveness.

When exploring resilience, we often think of big adversities that people face. Yet, what about the young people we minister to who have not faced great adversities? What about those who really do come from a nuclear family unit, where poverty is not an issue they come across, and they are academic high achievers coasting through life? How do we demonstrate and advocate for resilience for—and in conjunction with—them?

Ann Masten researches the science of resilience in children and young people.[20] Her research in Ordinary Magic explores what allows certain individuals to thrive and adapt despite adverse circumstances, such as poverty and trauma. She challenges the idea that resilient children are only those who face great adversities, and questions what happens to those who do not have such a high-profile case. She says:

> What began as a quest to understand the extraordinary has revealed the power of the ordinary. Resilience does not come from rare and special

qualities, but from the everyday magic or ordinary, normative human resources in the minds, brains, and bodies of children, in their families and relationships, and in their communities.

Perhaps the challenge for us is to find those moments of ordinary magic in our youth groups, churches and communities and also embrace the ordinary, not just the extraordinary, finding Christ at work in the daily grind as well as in corporate worship or healing services.

Think

- What might you do to create a space of safety and support?
- What might the role of mentors look like in your youth work/church?
- What does serving your local schools—both primary and secondary—look like? What do Purpose, Partner and Passion look like in your setting?
- How do you build topics such as suffering and forgiveness into the youth discipleship programme?

6 Final Reflections

As we conclude, we hope you have received a snapshot of the power resilience can play in faith-filled lives of the young people we seek to serve. We trust this writing has helped you to reflect on what building resilience in young people might look like within the context that you find yourself.

Our prayer from here on is for this booklet to be a contribution in equipping the communities that support young people as they themselves commit to a Christlike journey of building resilience.

By taking a holistic approach, and incorporating the young person's emotional, mental, physical and spiritual health, we can help young people to understand that God is interested in them as a whole person, and enable them to be the people that God created them to be, living life in all its fullness. If they do this and we help them on this journey, when they are faced with adversity, they may not only just survive, but also thrive.

As you reflect back on the five chapters of this booklet think about the areas we have considered.

Think

- What does resilience mean and why is it important?
- What does resilience look like?
- What makes and breaks resilience?
- How do I build resilience in young people?
- What role can churches play in the building of resilience in young people?

Which areas stand out as most important either to you personally or in your current area of practice? Our prayer is that in here are some areas that will support the 'Rebecca's' of your youth group, giving you tools which help equip both the young people you seek to serve, as well as yourself.

May the fluidity of resilience thread throughout your life and be in tune with the Holy Spirit, as well as those you minister to. As we collectively move forward may you lean into the discomfort, embrace the journey and exercise the muscle of resilience.

May it all be for the glory of God; to exalt him as we continue to serve in the lives of young people.

Notes

1 E Werner, 'Resilience in Development,' *Current Directions in Psychological Science*, American Psychological Society, 1995, 4, pp 81–85.

2 D Murphey, M Barry and B Vaughn, 'Positive Mental Health: Resilience,' *Child Trends*, 2013-3, pp 1–6.

3 T Newman, 'Promoting Resilience: A Review of Effective Strategies for Child Care Services,' (Exeter: CEBSS, 2002). Available at: https://nursingacademy.com/wp-content/uploads/2020/01/promotingresiliencenewman.pdf

4 B Brown, *Daring Greatly: How the Courage to be Vulnerable Transforms the Way we Live, Love, Parent and Lead* (New York: Gotham Books, 2012).

5 C Dweck, 'The Power of Believing That You Can Improve,' accessed 28 March 2021: https://www.ted.com/talks/carol_dweck_the_power_of_believing_that_you_can_improve/up-next

6 M Warner, *Joseph: A Story of Resilience* (London: SPCK, 2020).

7 Royal College of Psychiatrists, 'Surviving adolescence: for parents and carers,' (2017). Accessed 29 September 2020 at: https://www.rcpsych.ac.uk/mental-health/parents-and-young-people/information-for-parents-and-carers/surviving-adolescence-for-parents-and-carers

8 D Goleman, *Emotional Intelligence* (London: Bloomsbury, 1996).

9 N Bahr and D Pendergast, *The Millennial Adolescent* (Victoria: ACER Press, 2007).

10 Resilience Framework (Children and Young People) (Oct 2012). Adapted from Hart and Blincow, 2007, and available at: https://www.boingboing.org.uk/resilience/resilient-therapy-resilience-framework/

11 R Warren, *The Purpose Driven Life: What on Earth Am I Here For?* (Grand Rapids, MI: Zondervan, 2002) p 30.

12 The Youthscape Centre For Research: 'The Story. Statistics, Trends and Research For Youth Work.'

13 BBC ONE, *Songs of Praise*, 'Simon Thomas: I promised my wife I wouldn't give up on my faith.' Accessed 30 May 2018: https://www.bbc.co.uk/programmes/p068m1np

14 Office for National Statistics, 'Measuring National Well-being: Quality of Life in the UK, 2018.' Accessed 27 April 2018: https://www.ons.gov.uk/peoplepopulationandcommunity/wellbeing/articles/measuringnationalwellbeing/qualityoflifeintheuk2018

15 Young Minds, 'Coronavirus: Impact on Young People with Mental Health Needs, 2020.' Accessed 29 September 2020: https://youngminds.org.uk/about-us/reports/coronavirus-impact-on-young-people-with-mental-health-needs/

16 S M Southwick and D S Charney, *Resilience: The Science of Mastering Life's Greatest Challenges* (Cambridge University Press, 2012) p 115.

17 K E Powell and C Clark, *Sticky Faith* (Grand Rapids, MI: Zondervan, 2011).

18 H Dengate and K Murphy, Phase, 'Rethinking the Model,' Seminar presentation at School Work UK Conference (2019).

19 C Brauns, *Unpacking Forgiveness: Biblical Answers for Complex Questions and Deep Wounds* (Wheaton, IL: Crossway Books, 2008).

20 A Masten, 'Ordinary Magic,' American Psychologist Association, 56(3), 2001, pp 227–238.